Grolier
Album
Series

ALBUM OF THE GREAT WAR

Desmond Morton

Grolier Limited
TORONTO

Contents

Canadian Cataologuing in Publication Data

Morton, Desmond, 1937–
    Album of the Great War

(Grolier album series)
For use in schools.
ISBN 0-7172-1609-8

1. World War, 1914–1918—Canada—Juvenile literature.
2. Canada—History—1914–1918—Juvenile literature.*
I. Title.   II. Series.

D522.7.M67 1986   j940.3'71   C86-094323-2

1234567890   DWF   09876

Printed and bound in Canada

Introduction

More than any other single event in our history, the First World War changed our lives. In a series of crises that lasted five years, almost every idea Canadians shared in 1914, from the role of women to the role of government, was changed almost out of recognition. Half the young men of Canada joined the army. Many of them faced the horrors and dangers of war on the Western Front. Hundreds of thousands of Canadian women suddenly faced new jobs and experiences which women had never known before. When the war ended, they were no more willing than men to return to old ideas and old ways.

This is a book which will tell you something of the experiences Canadians shared in the war. It will tell you how the war came to involve Canada, why young men joined up, what young women experienced when they worked in munitions factories and, most of all, how the war affected all of us by its impact on a generation that is now almost gone.

Yet remember that Canada was only one country in the war. Most of the people in the world were involved, directly or indirectly, and people of all the heritages that now make up Canada will have their own special memories of the 1914–18 war. Most of the terrible fighting occurred in Europe, but the impact spread around the world, from China and the West Indies to Australia and Africa as much as to Canada.

Seventy years and more after that war, we see how cruel and futile it was. The enemies in that war are now respected allies. Because people tried to end all wars by crushing the losers of the First World War, they made a second World War almost inevitable. That was hidden from people at the time, just as our future is hidden from us. Can we learn from the past that hatred and cruelty only breed even more hatred and cruelty?

Thinking about the First World War, as this book does, opens the possibility of sharing the experience with parents, grandparents and friends. You may want to find photographs and diaries, old letters and newspapers and other family souvenirs. Why not ask older people what they remember of the war? Visit your local library or museum. Ask about county or provincial archives, where such records are kept.

When we understand more about the terrible experience of the First World War, we may ask ourselves who gained, who lost and why.

The Coming of War

In much of Canada, Monday, August 4, 1914 was a holiday. Crowds fled the heat to beaches, ball-parks and race-tracks, but others thronged outside newspaper offices, waiting for bulletins posted almost hourly. Hoarse-voiced newsboys hawked smudgy extra editions, rejoicing when excited buyers forgot to wait for change from a nickel. Wars were good for business.

All weekend there had been news of a European war. The great empires had called out their armies. Between the rumours and reports, Canadian newspapers gave readers a crash course on why the Great War had finally come.

It was a long, complicated story. Perhaps it began in 1870, when France was beaten by the disciplined soldiers of Prussia and her allies. Weaker than the German Empire that arose after 1870, the French made an alliance in 1894 with Russia. In turn, Germany made an alliance with the Austro-Hungarian Empire, a collection of nationalities, many of them eager to be free of their Hapsburg emperor, Franz-Josef. On June 28, 1914, Franz-Josef's grandson and heir was killed by a terrorist at Sarajevo.

Suddenly, with a terrifying inevitability, Europe's alliances found themselves at war. Serbians were blamed for the killing at Sarajevo. The Austrian Empire demanded a heavy penalty from Serbia. As defender of all Slavic people, including Serbs, the Russians prepared for war. On August 1, Kaiser Wilhelm II mobilized Germany's army to support Austria. France had to support Russia. Germany could not beat both of her neighbours at once. She would hold off the Russians while most of her armies raced west across neutral Belgium to overwhelm the French.

If Britain was at war, Sir Wilfrid Laurier had said in 1910, Canada was at war. But why would Britain get involved? Germany had once been a close ally; France and Russia were old enemies. However, Kaiser Wilhelm had decided to match Britain's naval strength with a German high seas fleet, and the countries became deadly rivals. There was a treaty, too, signed in 1830. Britain, France and Prussia had all agreed to protect Belgium. On August 1, Germany tore up that "scrap of paper." As German armies smashed their way into Belgium, the British sent an ultimatum to Berlin: withdraw by midnight, August 4, or the British Empire would declare war. The Germans ignored it.

The news that Britain was at war reached Ottawa at 8:55 P.M. The Minister of Militia, Colonel Sam Hughes, was delighted. So were many Canadians. Crowds packed the streets in cities across Canada, as much in Montreal and Quebec as in Toronto or Vancouver.

Why were Canadians so happy? Four terrible years later, they might wonder. In 1914, war

As the news flashed across the country, Canadians appeared united as never before. Even Henri Bourassa, the fiercely *nationaliste* editor of *Le Devoir*, declared that Canada must contribute "within the bounds of her strength, and by means which are proper to herself, to the triumph ... of the combined efforts of France and England."

"The people jammed every inch of space, vibrating with unrestrained enthusiasm at every display of what might be termed 'Britishism.' ... As each bulletin flashed its pregnant message, the crowds cheered and swayed as if possessed. Hats shot aloft, ten thousand throats boomed out a concentrated roar—a warning to the enemy, an inspiration to every soul in the British Empire. ... Up and down several principal thoroughfares a unique procession passed, leaving a storm of awakened feelings in its train. Some hundreds of men, waving the Union Jack and Canada's flag, with drums beating and rousing British airs stirring the atmosphere, marched along, an undeniable testimony of Canada's unswerving loyalty ...."

Toronto *Globe*, August 5, 1914

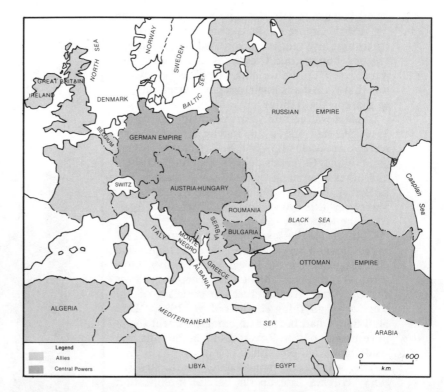

Prime minister since 1911, Sir Robert Borden was not a man of great flair or imagination. He was, however, an honest and intelligent man with an unwavering sense of duty and a remarkable amount of determination.

In September, cheering crowds happily thronged railway stations across Canada to give excited volunteers a gala send-off. Their ideas of war had been formed by bloodless peacetime manoeuvres and romantic paintings of flashing sabres and heroic charges. Nowhere in the popular imagery of war was there any hint of the agony, filth, stench and chaos awaiting across the Atlantic.

seemed an adventure. Not for a hundred years had the British Empire known a great war. Experts insisted that any modern war would be very short. History books told Canadians that the British were always on the winning side. The only worry was that Canadians might not get overseas in time to share in the fighting.

Canada was certainly not very ready for war in 1914. She had only a tiny regular army and a reserve, or militia, of 55 000. Still, Colonel Hughes had doubled Canada's defence spending. Artillery and other equipment poured into Canada as fast as British factories could produce it. Canadians made very little war equipment of their own, apart from the Ross rifle.

Colonel Hughes was the Ross's greatest admirer. It was a very accurate rifle and Hughes was an expert marksman. It was also a heavy, awkward weapon that failed to fire when it got even slightly dirty. Hughes forbade criticism of the Ross or of anything else he did. By 1914, "Drill Hall Sam" had become an embarrassment to the government of Sir Robert Borden, but the war made him a national hero.

After war began, many Canadians thirsted for glory. Hughes tore up the careful mobilization plan his staff officers had worked out and invited volunteers to meet at Valcartier, a sandy plain near Quebec. The government offered a force of 25 000 soldiers; by September, more than 32 000 men and 8000 horses had poured into Valcartier. Many came from Canada's militia regiments; even more were volunteers with no training. Most were recent immigrants from Britain. It was easier for them than for many young Canadians to abandon jobs or prairie homesteads. By October 3, Canada's first contingent had been loaded in ships. In these early months, almost all Canadians appeared united and excited by the war. At the same time, it was no longer so certain that the war would be over by Christmas. The German attack through Belgium had hurled French and British armies almost to Paris before a French counterattack at the Marne threw back the invaders. In October, at Ypres, Belgium, British divisions had barely held the line. By November, trenches stretched almost unbroken along the Western Front from the English Channel to the Swiss border. Meanwhile, a German army had destroyed a far larger Russian army at Tannenberg in East Prussia, showing the weakness of the Tsar's armies and the corruption of his generals.

The war would not be over by Christmas.

Kit inspection at Valcartier, September 1914. Commandeered by Colonel Hughes, an army of workmen had scurried to Valcartier and with astonishing speed laid out roads and drains, set up hundreds of tents and dozens of cookhouses, and built the biggest rifle range in the world.

"In great splendour like Napoleon," according to one recruit, a boastful and happy Sam Hughes spent September riding around Valcartier, promoting his cronies, berating his critics and struggling to pull some kind of order out of the chaos he had created.

Family goodbyes at Union Station, Toronto.

FOR DISCOVERY

1. How was the outbreak of war in 1914 greeted in your community? (You might find old newspapers in your local library or your county archives.)
2. Can you explain the enthusiasm of Toronto crowds in 1914? How do you think modern-day Canadians would greet the approach of war?
3. If Canadians were so enthusiastic about the war in 1914, why were most of the men at Valcartier found to be British-born?

Amid indescribable confusion, horses, equipment and over 30 000 men were somehow sorted out at the Quebec docks and loaded into 30 ships. The convoy sailed for England on October 3. On board the ships, accommodations for officers were reasonably comfortable; enlisted men slept in hammocks strung up at night over the meal tables and taken down in the morning.

Joining Up

By October 1915, the government had promised 250 000 soldiers for the Allied war effort. In his New Year's message for 1916, the prime minister, Sir Robert Borden, promised half a million men. Because Canada was suffering a severe depression in 1914, many men in the early contingents joined up to find work, but by 1915 there were jobs for all who wanted them. Still, the Canadian Expeditionary Force (CEF) met its target for volunteers.

It was not easy. Canada's militia regiments became a vast recruiting organization for the CEF. So did businesses, churches, schools and universities. Wealthy people gave the money to pay for recruiting posters. Most Canadians contributed to a Canadian Patriotic Fund to support soldiers' families.

Why did men join? Some were drawn by a sense of adventure, or a desire to escape from the boredom of school work or a job. Many felt a sense of duty as citizens. Often they followed brothers or friends. Teachers, clergy and patriotic associations told young men that they must be cowards if they did not join up. In some cities, women stood on street corners, pinning white feathers, the symbol of cowardice, on young men in civilian clothes. The government disapproved of "shaming" tactics but it left recruiting methods and expenses to local initiative.

In all, 258 CEF battalions were formed, though only 48 of them were actually needed for the Canadian Corps overseas. It seemed more attractive to join a new unit than to fit into an old one. Recruiters promised that friends who joined their battalion would serve together, all the way to Berlin. Some battalions offered Scottish or Irish traditions. Some wanted "sportsmen"; one Toronto battalion promised mothers that its men would never touch liquor.

The CEF wanted physically fit men between the ages of 18 and 45. About 30 000 youngsters lied about their age; so did as many others who were far too old. Thousands of men who were sick or disabled were passed by medical officers who were too busy, inexperienced or sympathetic to check properly. Who wanted to discourage patriotism? In fact, the young, the old and the unfit often broke down under army training, and only half the men who joined the CEF ever actually saw frontline service.

Soldiers wore a heavy wool tunic and breeches over a flannel shirt and cotton or woollen underwear. Army boots were stiff and heavy and it took many hours of marching to break them in. A heavy greatcoat served as raincoat or overcoat according to the season. On the march a soldier struggled under as much as 45 kilograms of equipment, spare clothing, water bottle, extra food, a rifle, bayonet and ammunition, to say nothing of whatever else staff officers deemed suitable.

As soldiers, most Canadians had everything to learn, from how to wind puttees—long strips of woollen cloth—around the ankle and calf so they would not come unwound to how to polish boots and brass buttons to a general's satisfaction. Seen here inspecting newly trained infantrymen at Valcartier is the Duke of Connaught, Governor General of Canada and Commander in Chief of the Canadian militia.

Toronto's mayor, Tommy Church, congratulates departing Italian reservists. Many young men who had come to Canada during the prewar wave of immigration were summoned back to serve in their homeland's forces.

The destination for Canada's mainly untrained First Contingent was Salisbury Plain in southern England. They arrived in warm sunshine but stayed through the wettest winter in memory. For four months, they marched and drilled, dug trenches and fired their rifles under constant driving rain. They also scrapped much of their Canadian-made equipment, including boots that dissolved in the mud and wagons that collapsed if fully loaded, and replaced it with sturdier British equivalents.

A refreshingly honest and practical appeal for men to join Canada's tiny wartime navy.

Recruiting rally, 1916.

Army life demanded new skills and attitudes. Army drill, with sergeants screaming orders mixed with crude personal insults, was intended to turn recruits into disciplined automata who would obey any command. Physical training and long, weary marches tried to harden men for the coming ordeal. Life in barracks robbed men of privacy while monotonous, badly cooked meals left them constantly hungry. They were eager to spend their pay of $1.10 a day on extra food as well as on a soldier's traditional comforts, beer and cigarettes.

Officers lived in a privileged world. Ordinary soldiers had to salute them, call them sir and never speak until spoken to. This grated on Canadians, who knew that most of their officers had little training and owed their rank to a few extra years of education and to social or political influence. Still, most soldiers accepted army discipline for the same reason they had joined up—a sense of duty. By 1917, most new Canadian officers were chosen from the ranks. They still bought their own, more elegant uniforms, ate in a separate "officers' mess" and had a soldier–servant or "batman" to look after their needs.

Soldiers who broke the army's rules could suffer punishments ranging from a few days of "CB"—confinement to barracks with extra drill and unpleasant duties—to death by firing squad for men found guilty of cowardice, running away from the enemy or striking an officer. During the war, 25 Canadians were shot by firing squad.

New soldiers saw the army from a worm's eye view. A man would know his own section—15 or so soldiers under a corporal—or his platoon, four sections commanded by a lieutenant, with a sergeant as a second in command. Four platoons formed a company under a captain or major, and four companies made up a battalion of 800 to 1000 men under a lieutenant-colonel. An infantry battalion, a cavalry regiment or an artillery battery became a soldier's home and extended family during the war. Old soldiers would never forget that they belonged to the 3rd "Torontos" or the 8th "Little Black Devils" from Winnipeg.

Soldiers knew that they were part of a huge military machine, mustering every kind of specialized military and civilian skill from mathematicians who controlled siege artillery or broke enemy codes, to the French and Belgian women who ran the baths and laundries where soldiers could strip away battlefield mud and lice.

Gradually a soldier came to know more about his military organization. His battalion was one of four in a brigade while three brigades, plus artillery engineers, medical, signals and army service corps units made up a division, commanded by a major-general. By March 1915, the Canadian first contingent had become the 1st Canadian Division in France. By September 1916, when the 4th Canadian Division reached the line, all the Canadians formed their own army corps. With almost 100 000 officers, nursing sisters and other ranks, the Canadian Corps had become one of Canada's greatest national institutions.

Recruiting posters and advertising appealed to pride, guilt or vengeance. Edith Cavell, an English nurse in Belgium, was shot by the Germans for helping British prisoners escape. Her death was considered a war crime though in fact the Germans had obeyed the harsh rules agreed to at pre-war conferences.

MURDERED By THE Huns
OCTOBER 12TH, 1915
MISS EDITH CAVELL
ENLIST IN THE 99th
AND HELP STOP SUCH ATROCITIES

COME INTO THE FINAL DRIVE WITH THE QUEEN'S UNIVERSITY HIGHLANDERS
OFFICER COMMANDING
Lt Col P.G.C. CAMPBELL
APPLY NEAREST RECRUITING STATION

LANGEMARCK
ST JULIEN
FESTUBERT
GIVENCHY
New names in Canadian history.
More are coming— Will you be there?
ENLIST!
Make us as proud of you as we are of him!

HOME SWEET HOME FOR YOU WE'RE FIGHTING
Captain Joe Lawson's Great Recruiting Song
WORDS OF CAPTAIN JOE LAWSON
MUSIC BY GORDON V. THOMPSON

Tom Longboat.

Canadian Indians were eagerly sought as volunteers for the CEF, and by 1918 an estimated 35 percent of Indian men of military age were enlisted. Among them was Tom Longboat, who had for a number of years been the champion long-distance runner in America.

Recruiting rally, Toronto, 1916. Canadians had by now suffered some heavy casualties and recruiting was petering out. If you were J.W. Geddes, the recruiter in the car, what sort of appeal would you make at this stage in the war?

FOR DISCOVERY

1. Find out about CEF battalions raised in your community during the First World War. What recruiting techniques did they use? How successful were they? What happened to local CEF units when they went overseas?
2. Find out what life was like for soldiers who joined the CEF. How has military life changed since 1914–18? Are there features that remain the same in the modern Canadian armed forces?

Western Canadian recruits training in Manitoba in 1915. The wide-brimmed straw hats, nicknamed "cow's breakfasts," were part of their uniform.

Staying Home

Most Canadians, of course, did not join the CEF. They went right on farming, selling insurance, keeping house, going to school or doing whatever they had done before August 1914. Sooner or later, though, the war changed their lives.

At first, the main impact was on spare time and money. Many men and women became personally involved in finding soldiers for the army, collecting money for soldiers' dependants, caring for the wounded when they came home from overseas. In the summer of 1915, when rumours spread that Canadian soldiers needed more machine guns, hundreds of thousands of dollars were contributed by companies, school children and ordinary citizens.

Such efforts were not always very efficient or well received. The government had already ordered as many machine guns as factories could produce. Soldiers' wives did not appreciate being treated as charity cases. Invalid soldiers got better faster in big hospitals with modern equipment and skilled nursing than in small convalescent homes.

Still, Canadians of all ages were bombarded by appeals to "do their bit." The Red Cross needed help making bandages and knitting socks. School children collected scrap metal, bottles and old newspapers. Later in the war, young people served as "soldiers of the soil," being released from school to help with farm work.

When war came in 1914, Canada was suffering from bad economic times, but by mid-1915, orders for uniforms, artillery shells and military equipment had set the economy buzzing. Everyone could find work. Employers raised wages to attract workers and passed on the costs to consumers. Men and women joined unions, and the labour movement grew in wartime as it never had before. Prices also began to soar. In the period 1916–19, the cost of living almost doubled. People who could not increase their incomes suffered severely.

Eventually, the war led to real shortages. The army and Canada's allies needed food. With so many men in uniform or taking well-paid jobs in munitions industries, farmers could not get their crops harvested and contingents of school children from the cities were not enough. When the United States entered the war in 1917, she needed almost all her coal exports for her own war industries. In the last year of the war, Canadians grew used to doing without all the food and fuel they would have liked.

Canada was a long way from the fighting but Canadians wanted to feel part of the struggle. Countless tag days were organized to raise money for patriotic and humane causes. Businessmen worked longer hours because sons or partners had

Since soldiers could hardly support their families on a private's pay of $1.10 a day, a Patriotic Fund was organized. Within three months it had raised $6 million.

"This woman I boarded with in Montreal had two young girls. . . . Her husband was overseas for four years, and she certainly never went anywhere. They led a pretty lonely life. She wasn't even allowed to have a telephone. She got $20 a month from her husband's pay and she got $20 a month from the Patriotic Fund. But this was a gift, it was charity, it wasn't from the Government. This was administered by a group of rich men's wives and if they found that a wife was running around, or if she was living beyond her means, they would cut her off. One of the ways she would live beyond her means was to put in a telephone, because obviously no soldiers' wife could afford a telephone."

Frank Bell, an electrician's apprentice in Montreal during the First World War. From Daphne Read (ed.), *The Great War and Canadian Society* (Toronto, 1978)

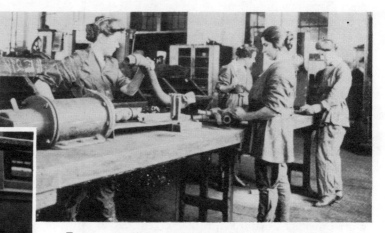

Newspapers and magazines were filled with patriotic messages, and every day seemed to produce a new song to "grip the heart" or raise the spirits.

Encouraged by rather patronizing publicity and specially designed costumes, women worked as "farmerettes" in harvesting crews, "conductorettes" on streetcars and in increasingly varied jobs in munitions and other industries. Their presence at the heart of the war effort, in non-traditional jobs, was part of a tide of change that affected every aspect of Canadian life.

joined the army. So did farmers. Women who had seen sons and husbands join the CEF waited with a terrible anxiety for the dreaded telegram bringing news of death or serious wounds.

Books, newspapers, magazines and the new silent movies all carried patriotic messages. The Allies were invincibly right; the Germans were unspeakably evil. Many atrocity stories were false or wildly exaggerated, but few in wartime doubted such fables as the Canadian sergeant crucified near Ypres. A Toronto school teacher, Harry Lee, who tried to tell his class that both sides might be justified, was reported by a couple of students. The school board fired him and Lee became the first Toronto teacher killed while serving with the CEF.

Before the war many Canadians had denounced war and militarism, but only a few brave men and women clung to such unpopular views once fighting began. Clergymen who had been pacifists now insisted that the war was a fiery furnace from which a purified Canada would emerge. Women who had demanded the vote because their sex was more likely to vote for peace now played a prominent role in patriotic causes, from recruiting soldiers to making munitions. It was because women promised to work for a greater war effort that the government gave many of them the vote in 1917.

Everyone was urged to buy bonds and war savings stamps. The finance minister, Sir Thomas White, believed it was fair to borrow the money for Canada's war effort. Why shouldn't future generations bear the cost of a "war to end all wars"? Wealthy Canadians proved to be very happy to buy the tax-exempt war bonds. So did their poorer fellow citizens. In 1917, when Victory Bonds were sold to people with small savings, the government hoped to raise $150 million. It collected $500 million.

Such borrowing contributed to inflation, but most Canadians blamed "profiteers" for soaring living costs. In 1916, pressure forced the government to tax business profits. A year later, Sir Thomas White announced "war income tax," to last only as long as the struggle. Canadians have been paying income tax ever since.

By the end of the war, the government had replaced voluntary organizations in many areas, from recruiting to military hospitals. Government inspectors controlled food and fuel supplies. Censors suppressed radical newspapers. Strikes were banned in 1918 and an "anti-loafing law" forced all men between the ages of 16 and 60 to hold a job. The government had taken over most of Canada's railways and it controlled the marketing of wheat and other basic products.

There was not much in Canadian life that was not affected by the war but the biggest, most lasting change was in the role of government. Four years of war taught Canadians what government could do. It was a hard lesson to forget.

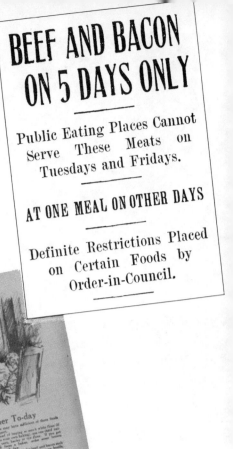

BEEF AND BACON ON 5 DAYS ONLY

Public Eating Places Cannot Serve These Meats on Tuesdays and Fridays.

AT ONE MEAL ON OTHER DAYS

Definite Restrictions Placed on Certain Foods by Order-in-Council.

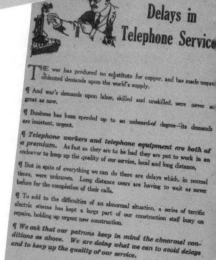

Delays in Telephone Service

The Bell Telephone Company of Canada

As fuel, food and other shortages grew serious late in the war, companies did their best to explain delays in service. Meanwhile, government agencies ordered fuelless days, advised housewives how to "save food and serve the Empire," deluged grocers and restaurant owners with regulations and threatened hoarders with jail sentences or fines.

Nova Scotia's Win-the-War Newspaper

THE HALIFAX HERALD
ALL THE NEWS.   HONEST VIEWS.   HONEST ADVERTISING.

Nova Scotia's Win-the-War Newspaper

FOUNDED FEBRUARY 14, 1875.   HALIFAX, CANADA, FRIDAY, DECEMBER 7, 1917.   VOLUME XLIII. NO 290.

HALIFAX WRECKED

More Than One Thousand Killed In This City, Many Thousands Are Injured And Homeless.

As the port from which convoys and most of Canada's soldiers departed, Halifax felt closer than most Canadian cities to the war. Nothing, however, prepared it for the morning of December 16, 1917, when a Belgian relief steamer collided with a French munitions ship. The greatest man-made explosion to that time devastated the city and much of neighbouring Dartmouth, took 1630 lives and left thousands more maimed and blind.

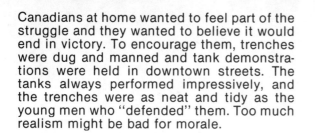

Canadians at home wanted to feel part of the struggle and they wanted to believe it would end in victory. To encourage them, trenches were dug and manned and tank demonstrations were held in downtown streets. The tanks always performed impressively, and the trenches were as neat and tidy as the young men who "defended" them. Too much realism might be bad for morale.

FOR DISCOVERY

1. Find newspapers or magazines published in your community during the First World War. How did the war affect daily life?
2. Why did direct government involvement replace much of the voluntary spirit as the war progressed? Why did some voluntary organizations, such as the Patriotic Fund and the Red Cross remain important?
3. How would the war have affected your life if you had been your present age in 1915?
4. Can you compare the impact on daily life of each of the two world wars? Were there differences? Why?

Enemy Aliens

Austrian prisoners in Lethbridge. Many internees were merely unemployed workers for whom local municipalities patriotically refused to provide relief.

When war came in 1914, not everyone in Canada cheered for Britain. Half a million people in Canada had their roots in Germany or the Hapsburg Empire. Many had arrived since 1901. International law made it clear that "enemy aliens"—men of military age and any who might try to help their homeland—could be interned or imprisoned. Among Canadians interned in Germany was a member of Parliament, Henri Beland, and a fine musician, Ernest Macmillan.

Ottawa had no plans for internment camps. They would be costly and unnecessary: the few Germans who wanted to fight for their Fatherland slipped into the United States and few of the Hapsburg subjects felt much loyalty. Many Canadians disagreed. One way to fight the war was to persecute neighbours. Governments and companies were forced to fire German-born employees. In Winnipeg, hamburgers were renamed "nips." Little boys "did their bit" by tormenting dachshunds, the small dogs cartoonists used to symbolize the enemy.

Public opinion forced the government to open internment camps. By the end of 1915, seven thousand men had been locked away in places that ranged from Kingston's old Fort Henry and a factory building in Amherst, Nova Scotia, to a bush camp at Kapuskasing. A few women and children were allowed to join "officer class" prisoners. A serious manpower shortage finally forced the government to release most of the Austro–Hungarians, but most of the Germans remained behind barbed wire.

Wartime prejudice was not limited to recent arrivals. The city of Berlin in western Ontario was a busy, prosperous place. No one could question its citizens' loyalty, but wartime hysteria drove people to do just that. To save the city's commerce, business leaders forced Berliners to change the name to Kitchener, after Britain's wartime commander. Such concessions did not appease hysterical patriots. They demanded that foreign-language newspapers be suppressed, that enemy aliens be compelled to work for $1.10 a day—a soldier's pay—and that they be deported at the end of the war. After 1917, when the Bolshevik government in Russia made peace with Germany, Russian-born Canadians became "enemy aliens" too.

At the end of the war, people in internment camps were deported. Kitchener did not return to its old name but it was a long time before its citizens forgot the wartime prejudice. Rumours of German spies and saboteurs proved groundless. The disasters blamed on them—the burning of the Parliament Buildings in 1916 or the Halifax Explosion of 1917—were due to human error. The "enemy aliens" of wartime once again became respected, valued fellow Canadians. Bitter memories faded but the prejudices that created them could always come back.

> *"Mr. Spade, who was a German, lived at two or four Jersey Avenue in Toronto. At the time, we lived at number fourteen. This happened after supper because I didn't see it happen. I overheard them talking about it. But a whole gang of men come around and got him and took him over, out on Clinton Street—that was only about a couple of hundred feet from his house—and they tarred and feathered him. Why, I don't know, though he never was in trouble of any kind that I know of. He was a carter, he had a horse and waggon. He worked steady and he never would drink or anything like that."*
>
> Howard Ainsworth, recalling wartime Toronto when he was ten years old. From Daphne Read (ed.), *The Great War and Canadian Society* (Toronto, 1978)

When a German submarine sank the passenger ship *Lusitania* on May 7, 1915, Canadians vented their outrage by attacking German-owned businesses. Seen here is the mob that gathered outside the Kaiserhof Hotel in Victoria. By the time it was dispersed, most of the windows had been smashed and the interior completely wrecked.

British Columbia miners went on strike rather than work beside potential enemies. To get the mines working, the government strung barbed wire, brought in tents and opened still more internment camps.

FOR DISCOVERY

1. The Great War has been called "the first people's war." Was hatred of the enemy a necessary emotion if ordinary people were to make wartime sacrifices? Did Canadians pay a price for their treatment of the "enemy alien"?
2. Do you think that the same kind of group hatred would grow in Canada again? How would you try to prevent it?

Otter Internment Camp, Yoho National Park, B.C. Internment orders were often based on doubtful evidence, but the courts refused to intervene. The War Measures Act, judges agreed, could not be questioned.

Materials of War

Sending soldiers overseas was an obvious contribution to the Allied war effort. So was the harnessing of Canadian production to the Allies' needs. No sooner was war declared than Ottawa announced that a million bags of flour—enough to fill 200 railway cars—would be given to the British people. Soon, Canada was exporting huge quantities of food, timber, and some munitions of war the country had never manufactured before.

In 1914, experts predicted a short war because no national economy could stand the strain for long. In Canada, the prewar depression got worse for a time. The two newest of Canada's three transcontinental railways were bankrupt. Many factories closed because people cancelled orders. Much of the new equipment sent with the First Contingent was designed to entice the Allies to place orders in Canada. Instead, much of it was scrapped as useless or of poor quality. The winter of 1914–15 was very hard for many Canadians.

Then the economy revived. After years of poor crops and low prices, Canada's 1915 wheat harvest broke records. The Allies bought huge quantities and asked for more. By 1918, prices more than doubled. Yields fell to dismal levels but farm incomes kept climbing. Greedy farming methods contributed to the dust bowl problems of the prairie provinces between the wars. With a chance to get rich quickly, farmers left the future to take care of itself.

Wheat was only one product in demand. Meat, fruit and timber all headed overseas at premium prices. Canadian minerals were in great demand, especially nickel, which was vital for hardening steel into armour plate. The big refinery at Sudbury was built to prevent American mine-owners from processing nickel in the United States (which was still neutral) and shipping it to Germany.

Before the war, Canada had bought her arms from Great Britain. A small factory at Quebec City made rifle ammunition and a few artillery shells. Another, nearby, produced the Ross rifle. Sam Hughes believed that Canada should get into the munitions business and he persuaded businessmen to form a Shell Committee and bid for British business. Though none of them had any idea of how to make artillery ammunition, they were willing to try and the British were desperate enough to issue contracts. Workers who had never done precision machining had to learn new skills. Tools were ordered from the United States. Promises were made. By the summer of 1915, Canada had over $150 million in orders—and had delivered only $5.5 millions' worth, all far behind schedule. The British were furious.

They, themselves, created a new organization in Canada called the Imperial Munitions Board (IMB). To take charge, they chose the businesslike bacon exporter, Joseph Flavelle. His energy and

Machining shells at the Cluff Ammunition Company in Toronto. Very few Canadian factories had ever done precision work, but by 1917 Canada was producing almost a third of the shells fired by the British forces.

Loading cartridge case with cordite charge.

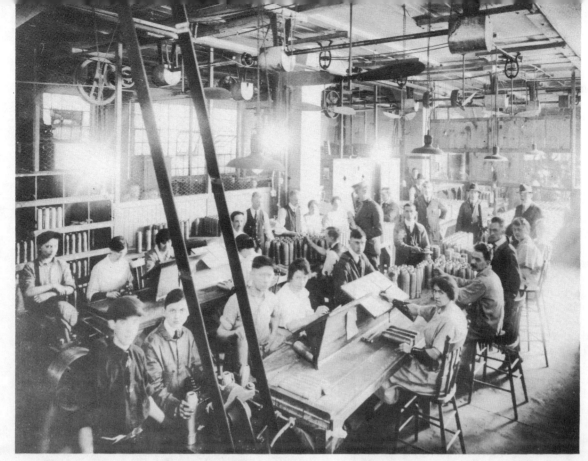

Final government inspection of 75 mm shells at a Montreal munitions factory.

What was it like to work in a munitions factory? Elaine Nelson remembered working in a shell factory in Toronto. She had been a singer in New York and a Red Cross volunteer:

"When the shell came I pushed a lever and the [conveyor] belt caused a knife to go just against the shell, and then would start to peel. The shell was turning all the time I pushed that lever against it. It would turn and you had to quickly knock off those jagged pieces before they got as far as your face, because they would just swing around, back and forth. . . . Oh yes, and right over there where this thing was—it looked like a great steel chisel—was this little tap. Just before you put your machine on, you turned this little tap so that it was pouring chemicals over that thing. And then you started. It poured all the time, and as these jagged pieces came out, it splashed this stuff. And that's what got all over us. It was really a miserable thing. . . if I hadn't been as healthy as I was, I'm sure I would have had pneumonia for sure. Because you had to go wringing wet like that across this long courtyard before you got to the place where you could change your clothes. It was bitterly cold. Your feet were frozen and the rest of you was just roasting because the machinery was hot."

From Daphne Rèad (ed.), *The Great War and Canadian Society* (Toronto, 1978)

Women's lunch room at the British Munitions Supply Company, Verdun, Quebec. Munitions firms came up with a variety of special services in order to induce women to work in their factories. Eventually, there were even promises of equal pay with men.

efficiency gradually produced results. He picked able managers, gave them authority and backed them up when contractors failed. By 1917, the IMB had become the biggest business Canada had ever seen, with 600 factories and a quarter of a million workers, 40 000 of them women. As well as millions of artillery shells, it was making brass casings, explosives and, eventually, cargo ships, training airplanes and flying boats.

Production from the IMB helped Canada pay for its war effort. The business helped keep the struggling railways financially afloat. By 1916, however, the British had spent all they could possibly afford on Canadian shells. Fortunately for Flavelle, Canadians had loaned hundreds of millions of dollars more than the government needed for its own purposes. Some of the surplus was used to keep the IMB going. Then, in 1917, the United States entered the war, providing a rich new market for Canadian munitions. Flavelle's salesmen found that the Americans needed everything Canadian factories could produce. The IMB stayed in business until the end of the war. Then, even faster than it was built, Flavelle dismantled it. He did not believe that governments in peacetime should run factories.

Men and women had worked in factories before the war but the IMB factories were a new experience. By custom, metalwork had always been reserved for men. A desperate shortage of manpower forced the board to ignore prejudices and to use women's skills wherever possible. Flavelle's managers found that women could do hundreds of jobs as well as men. Of course, the IMB would not carry the experiment so far as to pay women as much as the men they replaced, though women munition workers earned far more than in "traditional" female occupations. While much of the IMB's work was too specialized to have much postwar application, hundreds of thousands of men and women learned new industrial skills. One educator declared that wartime manufacturing had changed the scale of accuracy from the foot ruler to the micrometer.

Wartime production in factories and on the farm also spread prosperity to many working people. While prices rose, so did wages, and full employment meant that even elderly or disabled family members could find a job. Amid genuine shortages of food and fuel, particularly in the last years of the war, were new signs of affluence. Automobiles in 1914 had been playthings for the very rich; by 1919, car registrations had risen to 341 316, up from 69 598 in 1914. Huge profits from his wartime bacon business helped make Sir Joseph Flavelle very rich and led Canadians to sneer at him as "His Lardship" after he was given a title, but a great many of his fellow citizens had also been enriched by the war.

FOR DISCOVERY

1. Find out how your community or region contributed to supplying the war effort during the First World War. Was there a lasting impact on the community and its economy?
2. How did Canada pay for her war effort in 1914–18? Are Canadians still bearing the costs?
3. Mark Irish, Imperial Munitions Board, to the Chief Press Censor, October 17, 1916:

   "We are beginning to use female labour in Munition Factories on night shifts as part of our programme regarding the dilution of labour. It is conceivable, but not probable, that some of these women or girls might be actually, or in imagination, interfered with on the streets while going to, or coming from, the place of employment. While of course no effort should be spared to avoid such occurrence, nor to exact the fullest punishment, yet having regard to the National cause, I submit that Press comments upon such an incident, should one occur, would be most unfortunate, as possibly producing a prejudice against the use of women in projective production."

   What precisely is the IBM's Director of Employment asking the Chief Censor to do and why? Was this a reasonable request?

When German U-boats threatened the sea lanes, the Imperial Munitions Board turned to ship-building. By the end of the war, contractors and the board's own national factories were also producing airplanes, flying boats, chemicals and explosives.

Women work at building lifeboats in Baddeck, Nova Scotia.

Building a Curtiss flying boat. Flying boats were used for anti-submarine patrol.

In 1915, the finance minister nervously sought $50 million from Canadians to finance the war effort. He got $100 million. Later bond issues also brought in far more than expected, and by 1919 individuals and corporate investors had bought $2 billion worth of victory bonds.

Trench Warfare

While some Canadian soldiers joined the fighting in December 1914, most of the Canadian Contingent only went to France in March 1915 just in time to help in the desperate battle at Ypres in April. A second division followed in September, a third and fourth in 1916. Canadians saw action when the fighting had taken its grim shape as trench warfare.

Like economists, most generals had believed that the war would be short. They were wrong, though it cost France alone a million men to find out. Machine guns, barbed wire and artillery favoured defence, not attack. To survive, soldiers had to burrow like moles. By the end of 1914, two long sets of trenches faced each other across a narrow strip of mud, wire, wrecked buildings and fragmented human bodies. There, more than three hundred thousand Canadians would experience war. One in six would die.

Trenches began as scrapes in the ground, dug by desperate soldiers. By the time Canadians arrived, the lines had become complex fortifications. Ideally, they stretched in a dog-tooth pattern across the landscape. Each "traverse" was only a few metres long so that an enemy shell would do limited damage. The dirt walls were shored up by sandbags, boards and corrugated iron. Above ground, a sandbagged parapet protected soldiers who stood guard, peering into no-man's land through a dense tangle of barbed wire. Behind the front line were reserve and support trench lines, connected by winding communication trenches. Well-hidden listening posts in front of the forward line, sniper posts, where crack shots waited for hours to bring death to a careless enemy and heavily sandbagged machine gun posts completed the defences. Behind the trench lines, batteries of field guns waited to shatter any enemy attack or to punish the opposing trenches. Farther behind, heavier guns concentrated on blasting enemy artillery.

Diagrams of trench warfare suggest a neat, sanitized order Canadians never knew. In northern France and Belgium, British lines ran through flat, dreary landscape, marked by industrial towns, coal mines and farms. Rain flooded the trenches and turned the ground into a thick, gluey mud.

At the front, routine was reversed: the night was for work; daytime was for rest. At dawn and at dusk, the likeliest time for an enemy attack, everyone *stood-to* for an hour, peering nervously into the gloom. After dark, working parties headed back to collect food, water, ammunition and supplies. The journey, in pitch darkness, might take all night. Others repaired the day's damage to the trench. A few, faces blackened, armed with clubs, knives and grenades, headed cautiously out through a gap in the barbed wire to patrol no-man's land or to try to capture a German prisoner

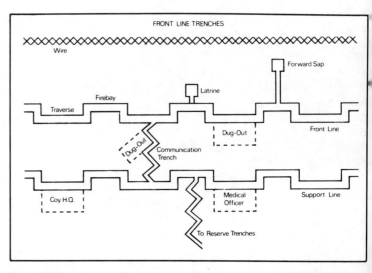

FRONT LINE TRENCHES

Wire
Forward Sap
Latrine
Firebay
Traverse
Dug-Out
Front Line
Dug-Out
Communication Trench
Support Line
Coy H.Q.
Medical Officer
To Reserve Trenches

Sniping through a "port hole" between the sandbags. There was sure to be an enemy sniper doing exactly the same thing, and the first lesson a soldier learned in the trenches was to keep his head down.

These Grenadier Guards from Montreal were among the first Canadians to reach the trenches in 1915.

Billy Bishop, the great Canadian air ace, could see the trench war from the sky.

"For the first time I saw the front line as it really was, mile upon mile of it. Now running straight, now turning this way or that in an apparently haphazard and unnecessary curve. The depth and complexity of the German trench system suprised me. No-man's land, much wider in places than I had realized from any map, looked like a long-neglected race-course by reason of the distinctive greenness of its bare but relatively undisturbed turf. Far behind, in enemy territory, I saw factories with smoking chimneys and pleasantly normal villages."

From Dennis Winter, *Death's Men*
(London, 1978)

Resting after a heavy night's work. Exhausted soldiers found that they could sleep in a puddle of water, standing up or even on the march.

Soldiers spent perhaps two weeks at a stretch in the trenches, alternating every three of four days between front and reserve lines.

Gas masks became a regular part of a soldier's equipment after the gas attack at Ypres. Steel helmets were issued in 1916 as a result of many losses from head wounds.

for the information he could give. The slightest sound might bring a rush of machine-gun fire, an artillery barrage and a sky lit up by flares and rockets.

At dawn, cold, weary men gathered for stand-to. Afterwards officers might issue the famous "S.R.D."—service rum, diluted—that burned like liquid fire. Soldiers were still needed for work and to stand guard, but there would be a few hours for food, cigarettes and sleep. Good trenches might have deep dugouts where men would be safe from anything but a direct hit. More often, soldiers bundled themselves in their great-coats and slept on the trench floor or on narrow shelves cut out of the trench wall. Rations arrived in sandbags, sugar tied in one corner, loose tea leaves in the other. Cans of stew or corned beef and the notorious plum and apple jam would be piled in. Army bread or hard, dry biscuit was on top.

The enemy and nature did all they could to make trench life a misery. Within days of reaching France, soldiers were infested with lice. Huge rats prowled the trenches, devouring food and dead bodies. The sickly-sweet stench of death and of human filth overpowered feeble efforts at sanitation. Poison gas, first used against the Canadians at Ypres in 1915, could be countered by gas masks, but both sides invented new and more terrible agents. Mustard gas, which left terrible blisters on the skin and lungs, was deliberately designed to injure rather than kill. Most soldiers agreed that artillery bombardments were the most terrifying experience of all in the trenches. As the earth trembled and shook, even the bravest could break down.

Even a short time in the trenches cost a battalion a few dozen casualties. After a couple of weeks—few could have survived the fear and the physical misery much longer—soldiers would march back to rest, perhaps in billets in French farms or villages, sometimes to the continued misery of rain-sodden tents. They might enjoy a bath in the vats of an abandoned brewery and a change to clean, if ill-fitting underwear. Once at rest, generals and officers would again insist on drill, saluting and polished brass buttons. Some soldiers would be sent on courses, perhaps to train to be officers, perhaps to master the succession of new weapons and tactics with which experts hoped to break the stalemate. There was little time for leave or real rest. Perhaps once a year, Canadians could hope for a week in England. Officers went more often. Otherwise, recreation was limited to a nearby *estaminet* or tavern where the staple for hungry soldiers was fried eggs and potatoes. For entertainment, battalions and then divisions organized their own shows. The most famous was the 3rd Canadian Division's troupe, the Dumbbells.

All too soon, the rest would be over. Soldiers would struggle into their heavy equipment and pick up their rifles, and the battalion would begin the long weary march back to the ordeal of the trenches.

A column of mud-bespattered Canadians returning from the trenches at the Somme, 1916.

Somehow soldiers managed to keep their sense of humour and laugh at their hardships. When at rest behind the lines, they learned to shut their minds to the grim realities of the trenches and enjoy whatever opportunities their rest billet had to offer. That might be no more than a bath and dry clothes, but for the lucky ones, there might be an appetizing meal in a French tavern or a performance by the Dumbbells.

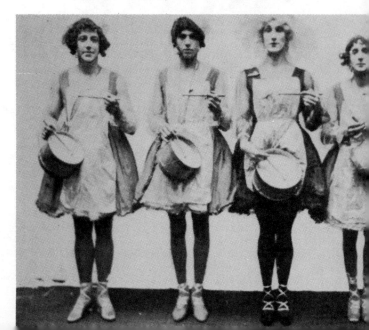

A soldier with an Alberta battalion, Private Donald Fraser, described an artillery barrage from the sending end:

"After passing through Dickebusch we literally threaded our way through a maze of batteries. On either side of us came blinding flashes from the guns and report following report seemed to rend the heavens. The noise was that of a hundred thunder claps. The air was seething with the whiz of shells. Every portion of our vicinity was enveloped in momentary flames and when a salvo went off, it almost burst our ear drums."

From R.H. Roy (ed.), *The Journal of Private Fraser 1914–1918* (Victoria, 1985)

Men of the 22nd Battalion rest in a shell hole on their way to the front line.

A Canadian soldier captured this photograph of his German counterparts enjoying themselves with wine and song. Soldiers rarely saw the enemy.

FOR DISCOVERY

1. Imagine that you had survived your first day in the trenches. Write a description of the experience for your family. Are there things a soldier might prefer not to tell his family?
2. See if you can find copies of letters real Canadian soldiers wrote home from the Front in the First World War. What sort of a picture do they give?
3. Why were so many military experts wrong in predicting how war would develop in 1914? Do you think that the experts could be wrong again?

A few Canadians scrounge a cup of tea at a field kitchen just behind the front lines at Hill 70.

Over the Top

The war could not be won by soldiers cowering in their trenches. The enemy had to be driven back. The first two years showed that it would not be easy. Only by mid-1916 had the shell factories given the British the mountains of ammunition they needed to even hope for success.

For a week at the end of June 1916, British guns poured a million and a half shells on German trenches at the river Somme. At 7:30 A.M. on July 1, 80 000 soldiers rose to attack. By nightfall, 57 570 of them lay dead or wounded. The little Newfoundland battalion lost 684 of its men; 310 of them were dead. All that summer, the British kept attacking. In September, it was the turn of the Canadian Corps. By then, tactics had improved. Artillery shells fell just in front of the attackers so that Germans could not clamber out of deep dugouts and open fire with machine guns. "Tanks," huge, lumbering monsters on caterpillar treads, could crush barbed wire and enemy machine-gun posts with equal ease.

That was the theory. Without wireless to control the guns, the planned barrages got far ahead of the infantry—or stopped and destroyed their own troops. Everything about tanks, from the steering to the transmission, broke down easily and often. Few reached the battlefield. Behind the lines, during a "Big Push," marching soldiers, horse-drawn supply wagons and convoys of trucks and ambulances created hopeless traffic jams on the narrow roads. An even worse problem was getting men and supplies forward across the shell-swept muddy morass of the battlefield.

Everything depended on the infantry. What was it like to wait for days under the earth-shaking, deafening nightmare of an artillery barrage? Men had plenty of time for their thoughts. Who would escape death or terrible wounds? Would some officer have the courage to cancel an attack if it was hopeless? Would a flanking unit fail, leaving its neighbouring battalion to be destroyed? At dawn, men would prepare themselves, collecting extra ammunition and grenades, a fresh water-bottle, a white cotton bag with food, a rolled groundsheet.

Then it was Zero Hour. Officers signalled and soldiers swarmed "over the bags" into the open, feeling naked as they formed a rough line and began to advance. Officers and sergeants would try to keep the line straight and moving at an even pace. Survivors would recall a dreamlike feeling of immunity from danger after the first panic. Soldiers often acted as though they were under some powerful drug, performing acts of heroism and self-sacrifice—and sometimes of cowardice—that they could not remember afterwards.

This mood was followed by an overwhelming fatigue as soldiers' bodies made up for the surge of adrenalin. The surviving attackers, often leaderless, always exhausted, faced a storm of German artillery and then waves of counter-attacking Ger-

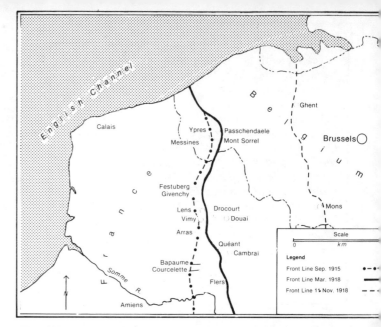

The Western Front.

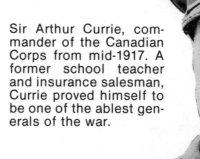

Sir Arthur Currie, commander of the Canadian Corps from mid-1917. A former school teacher and insurance salesman, Currie proved himself to be one of the ablest generals of the war.

Lieutenant Grant remembered what it was like waiting for an attack at the Somme:

"I gave the men a good look. They seemed more or less in a trance. Their eyes were glassy and their faces white as chalk. But the way their mouths were set gave me confidence. One or two shook hands. An old private, lying down by a very young corporal, suddenly kissed him on the cheek and then lay down again flat. My orderly behind me tugged my ankle. I could see he had something to say but the din was terrific. He looked very excited. I noticed the beads of sweat all over his face. Putting his mouth to my ear, he yelled, 'Til the very last, Lieutenant.' I remember patting him on the shoulder."

From Dennis Winter, *Death's Men*
(London, 1978)

The battlefield after a Canadian charge.

Soldiers hurriedly set up their machine guns in a shell hole during the attack on Vimy Ridge, April 1917.

The taking of Vimy Ridge. As the Canadians advanced, parties of Germans left their dugouts, only too glad to surrender.

man infantry. It was impossible for generals to find out what was happening and send help. The marvel was not that attacks so often failed but that any succeeded. "If hell is as bad as what I have seen at Courcelette," wrote Colonel Thomas Tremblay, "I would not wish my worst enemy to go there." Tremblay's French Canadians and a Nova Scotia battalion took Courcelette and somehow endured the hell.

Canadians learned from the Somme and their other bitter experiences. Vimy Ridge was the proof. On Easter weekend, 1917, the Canadian Corps had to take the German stronghold. For months in advance, Canadians piled supplies, dug tunnels and even learned how to operate any German guns they might capture. Behind the lines, a huge area was marked off as a replica of the Ridge. Canadian units rehearsed and rehearsed. Airplanes pinpointed German targets. When the artillery bombardment came, it was unmatched in accuracy and weight. Still, the Canadian victory at Vimy cost 10 602 casualties, 2598 of them dead. By Great War standards, the price was small.

Vimy set the Canadian style: long careful preparation, a huge weight of shells to crush the enemy, a limited objective so that the gains could be protected from counter-attack. At Hill 70, that summer, the Corps' Canadian commander, Sir Arthur Currie, took advantage of the fact that the Germans would try to retake what had been captured. He made sure that the Canadian attackers were specially well prepared. Wave after wave of German counter-attack was destroyed by Canadian artillery and machine guns.

In October 1917, the British commander insisted that the Canadians rescue a British offensive that had blundered disastrously into the waterlogged swamp of Passchendaele. Currie believed the attack was foolish; he knew it would cost sixteen thousand dead and wounded. As a soldier, he obeyed, but again he insisted that every possible preparation be made. When the terrible conditions slowed his men down, he refused to be hurried. Soldiers waited, rested or were replaced by fresher men. Finally, at the terrible cost Currie had predicted, the Canadians succeeded. It could have been far worse.

For ordinary soldiers at the front, that was small comfort. They could see war only from their platoon or company. Each attack meant only that they or those who had become their closest friends would face death or terrible wounds. The huge casualties were not spread through the army; they fell on the front-line infantry. Half or three-quarters of a platoon might be killed or wounded. Officers had an even shorter life expectancy than their men. Infantry lieutenants lasted, on average, only five or six weeks at the front.

This was the awful ordeal Canadian soldiers faced. They saw no alternative and they stuck to their dreadful task.

Men, supplies, even artillery guns disappeared in the deep mud and the flooded shellholes of the battlefield at Passchendaele. One veteran's comment many years later: "Passchendaele? It was the worst place in the world."

Major Georges Vanier. During the attack on the German Hindenberg line in August 1918, every officer of the 22nd Battalion was killed or wounded, including Major Vanier, a future governor general of Canada.

A squadron of Fort Garry Horse on the Cambrai front, 1917.

"Somewhere in France" is all the military censors would allow anyone to know. Canadians remembered the devastation as the first big shock of the war. Soon, they took it for granted.

FOR DISCOVERY

1. Find out, from newspapers of the time, how Canadians learned about the big offensives of the First World War. Were they told the truth? Why?
2. Why did soldiers go "over the bags" in the face of such terrible dangers? What aspects of army life helped them?

At Cambrai, 324 tanks broke through the German line, but 179 of them were out of action by nightfall as a result of breakdown, enemy shell fire or simply getting stuck in the mud.

Mass burial, Doullens, France, 1918. Every effort was made to provide a proper burial for the fallen and to mark and register their graves. It was, of course, not always possible, and almost a third of the Canadian dead had no known grave.

A "Blighty"

Apart from an end to the war, there were only two ways to escape from the horrors of the front lines: death or a serious wound. Soldiers talked wistfully of a "blighty," a wound serious enough to get them back to "Blighty"—British army slang for England. The Canadians lost 51 948 killed in action and 138 166 men wounded or gassed.

The Canadian Army Medical Corps was small in 1914, but many of Canada's best doctors had joined the militia in peacetime and no branch of the CEF was better prepared. By the end of the war, about a fifth of all Canadian doctors had joined the army and a quarter of Canada's registered nurses, 2854 women, had served as nursing sisters. Other women volunteered as ambulance drivers and as nurses' aides. University medical schools organized field hospitals. Medical researchers worked in army laboratories, trying to find answers to poison gas, gangrenous wounds and the mysterious problem of "shell shock."

Soldiers in the 1914–18 war were luckier than their fathers. Even in the South African War, 1899–1902, diseases had killed thousands of soldiers. Typhoid fever, the biggest killer, and tetanus, the feared "lockjaw" which had killed many wounded in earlier wars, could be stopped by innoculation. Smallpox, another killer of armies, was stopped by compulsory vaccination. The new war brought new problems. Soldiers standing for days in mud and icy water suffered "trench foot." Doctors found that regular changes to clean, dry socks could solve the problem. "Trench fever" left thousands weakened and out of action; medical researchers traced the source to one of the tiny fleas that infested soldiers' clothing. The CEF reported 350 000 cases of sickness but only 5000 died. Still, there was much that doctors did not know. Most of the 2000 Canadian soldiers who died from pneumonia would now be saved by antibiotics.

Soldiers might want a "blighty"; getting one was another matter. Helpless wounded men in no-man's land might wait for hours before help could come. Their moans or screams might draw comrades into suicidal rescue attempts. In big attacks at the Somme or Passchendaele, it would take days before rescue parties could reach all the thousands of wounded.

If a soldier could, he would pull out his field dressing and bandage his wound. Then, if he could, he would struggle back to safety. Helpless men would be carried by battalion stretcher bearers. In the sodden mud, it might take relays of six carriers to remove a single casualty.

Because movement caused many deaths from shock, wounded were carried in stages. The first stop was a battalion aid post where a busy doctor could do no more than check bandages and inject morphia to ease pain. At an advanced dressing station farther back, the weary bearers loaded

Helping the wounded in after the taking of Vimy Ridge, May 1917.

A member of a rescue party administers first aid to a Canadian wounded in the advance east of Arras, September 1918.

A German shell bursts close to an advanced dressing station at Vimy. "That experience," Roger F. Clarke later wrote, "was far worse than merely being wounded, for I was so afraid that now I was decently wounded, I'd get killed before I could get out."

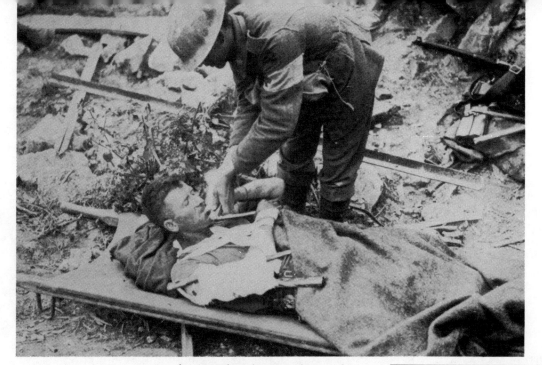

A stretcher bearer does what he can to make his patient comfortable at a battalion aid post before heading back for another one. During and after a big attack like Vimy or Passchendaele, stretcher bearers might work with little sleep or food for days on end.

Canadian nurses served in England, Belgium, France, Greece, Egypt and Russia. Of the 2400 who went overseas, 18 were killed by bombs or submarines and 15 died of disease.

A Canadian medical officer was sent up to take charge of an aid post during the battle of Passchendaele. This is part of his report:

"Very heavy shelling was going on and continued almost incessantly through the night. Outside the aid post I found lying on stretchers about 9 or 10 very severe stretcher cases, chests and abdomens, compound fractures, spinal injuries etc. They were quite unprotected from shell fire, the night was cold, almost freezing, and many of them had no great-coats. Apparently they had received no treatment except that of the stretcher bearers, and no attempts to treat them, relieve their pain or warm them was being made. Going inside I found about 25 patients, all stretcher cases but not on stretchers and huddled together. There was no room even to walk between them . . . . I found Capt. _____, M.O. --th Bn. huddled up under the table with a ground sheet covering his head. He had an aphonia which had come on suddenly which I think was hysterical . . . . The noise outside was terrific, shells bursting everywhere and the candle which lighted the place was frequently blown out by the explosions."

their casualty in an ambulance, to be jolted mercilessly along cobbled roads to a casualty clearing station. There, for the first time, surgeons could operate on the wound. Nursing sisters not only organized care but brought an air of civilized normality that almost every wounded man remembered. Then men were loaded on ambulance trains to be carried to hospitals.

Many of the wounded died. Shock from broken bones grating together or from loss of blood killed many. Blood transfusions were still experimental and there was no system of typing blood. Even worse was "gas gangrene." Years of farming filled the soil with micro-organisms. Bullets or shell fragments carried scraps of filthy uniform and mud deep into wounds. At first, doctors believed that the body could cure itself. Then, when soldiers died in terrible pain from the balloon-like swelling, they learned to cut away all the affected flesh and to plug the gaping hole with bandages soaked in powerful disinfectant. Even bullet wounds that might have healed in a few months would take years to disappear.

Some wounds were invisible. As the war continued, more and more men suffered from what doctors at first called "shell shock," but a later war would call "battle exhaustion." Generally, doctors insisted that such men were merely cowards and should be punished until they went back to fighting. The fact that doctors did not understand the problem did not keep them from being very definite in their diagnosis and cure.

Yet, for all they did not know, doctors, nurses and orderlies did their best to ease the terrible toll of death and suffering on the battlefield. Canada's first Victoria Cross—the highest decoration for bravery—went to Captain Fred Scrimger, a Montreal doctor at the Battle of Ypres who risked his life again and again to protect his patients.

At the end of the war, about 60 000 Canadians had earned disability pensions from wounds or disease, but only about a quarter of them were judged to be seriously disabled. Over the years, many more felt the effects of wounds and sickness. Saddest of all were those for whom the terrible emotional strain of war in the trenches had led to nervous collapse. The general belief that they could cure themselves by "behaving like a man" meant that there was no treatment, no pension and no respect. They were among the most pathetic of war casualties.

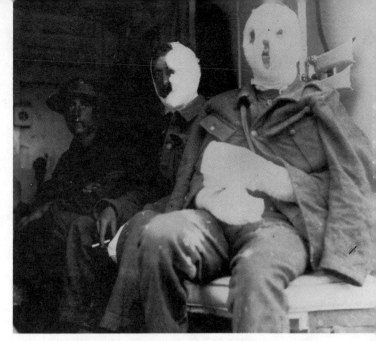

Victims of mustard gas being taken by ambulance to a casualty clearing station.

Sergeant Thomas Geggie wrote this cheerful report to the Toronto *Daily Star* in 1917 from a hospital in England.

"A word about plugs. Now, I have not the slightest objection to plugs as such. I have on occasion found it useful as a retainer of water in my bath. On a very wet day in the trenches, . . . a plug in the shape of tobacco was not to be despised, but when the plug is composed of about a yard of saturated lint, and this is plugged into a cavity in one's leg about the size of an ordinary breakfast cup, take it away. There is just one thing in this world more painful than plugging a wound, and that is unplugging a wound. The withdrawal of a plug caused me to emit my first, and only hospital yell. It was a good yell, though perhaps I say it who shouldn't. I was immediately told that it was a most ungentlemanly thing to do; that as an old soldier and a non-commissioned officer of some standing, I ought to show a better example. From that day I resorted to the time-honoured expedient of chewing holes in my leather belt during the plugging and unplugging."

An ambulance driver changes a tire on her Canadian Red Cross ambulance.

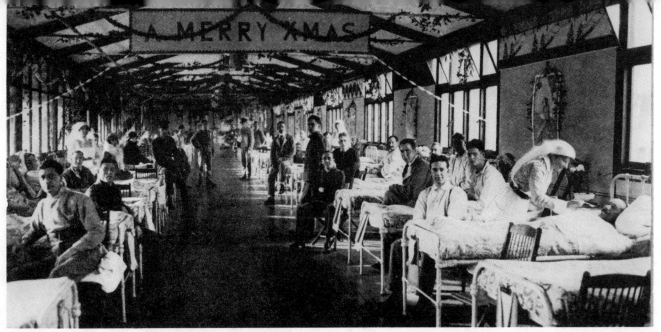

Christmas in a Canadian hospital ward in England.

Convalescent Canadians at a leave centre in England. Canadian doctors, nurses and hospital staffs managed to return more than three-quarters of the wounded to duty. Many Canadians were wounded several times.

FOR DISCOVERY
1. If you were the doctor in the quoted passage, what would you have done?
2. Find out about the medical advances that benefited soldiers in the Second World War, Korea and Vietnam. Has war become more, or less, "humane"?
3. One Canadian division (the 1st) insisted that it had no cases of shell shock because it would not tolerate them. Remembering that the army needed to have men to fight in terrible conditions, how would you have handled the problem?

Between meetings of the Imperial War Cabinet in 1917, Sir Robert Borden spent every possible moment visiting Canadian wounded. The sacrifices they had made convinced him that conscription was not only necessary but a moral duty.

In the Air

The Great War saw many new inventions, from flame-throwers and poison gas to the huge, lumbering "tanks." None was as dramatic as the airplane.

Certainly armies had used balloons before, and it was the big, clumsy observation balloons, with their sharp-eyed watchers, that forced front-line soldiers to do their day's work at night. Airplanes, however, were brand new to war. From the first days, they were sent over the enemy's lines to spot signs of movement. Soon, they could guide the artillery to a target.

At first, the clumsy "box-kites" were unarmed. Pilots had enough to do to keep them flying. By 1916, aircraft builders were designing special planes as "fighters." A German inventor devised a gear so that a pilot could fire a machine gun straight ahead without hitting a propellor blade. The Germans also had better engines, metal covering for the aircraft body and even armour to protect the pilot. The Allies followed as fast as they could. So quick was development that the very best planes were often out-dated in six months.

The first airplane flight was in 1902. Only in 1910 had Britain agreed that airplanes might be useful in war. Canada's Militia Department solemnly rejected them: "not enough is known about them," said an official. When war came, Sam Hughes refused to approve a Canadian air force. Yet many young Canadians wanted to fly. Because the British insisted that would-be pilots already have training, an American, Glenn Curtiss, set up Canada's first flying school outside Toronto. Even the best instructors were still learning the mysteries of trying to recover from a spin and how to keep the plane from stalling as it approached to land.

Soldiers in the trenches envied the freedom of flyers, and certainly pilots lived very comfortably behind the lines. They made up for it in the air. Early airplanes were hard to fly, even for experienced pilots. British and Canadian pilots had very few hours' training. Once in the air, pilots headed west over the German lines. British officers insisted on regular patrols to show "the offensive spirit." The Germans preferred to wait patiently, to swoop down from the rear—a pilot's blind spot. The odds were that a pilot would not survive his first 20 flights. The British forbade parachutes—the weight would have made British planes even slower than they were—and a pilot went down with his plane. Since the pilot sat on the gas tank, he would be the first to know if the fuel exploded.

By 1917, the British flying services were desperate for pilots. Younger and less experienced men were sent to the squadrons, only to die all the sooner. An offer by Joseph Flavelle and the Imperial Munitions Board to build airfields and train pilots in Canada was eagerly accepted. The Cana-

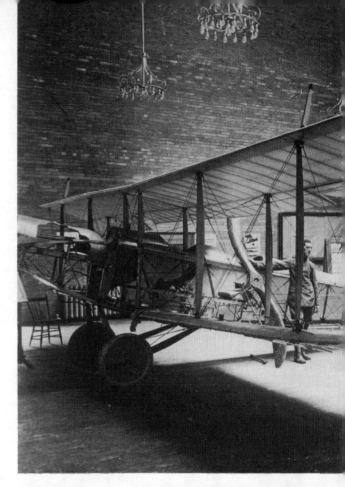

During the early years of the war, most Canadian pilots trained at their own expense and went to England to enlist. The new British flying services welcomed them, and by 1917 Britain was vigorously recruiting and training pilots and mechanics in Canada.

His majesty King George V visits an airfield in France.

Royal Air Force Sopwith Camels in France, July 1918. In no area did technology move faster or with more deadly consequences. Every few months the best aircraft in the skies was outclassed by a better design or a stronger engine, with the Germans usually in the lead.

Aerial photographs provided valuable information about enemy movements and defences.

As airplanes would improve over the course of the war, so would the anti-aircraft guns used against them.

dians already with the Royal Flying Corps and the Royal Naval Air Service had a fine reputation. The British were eager for more. Young Canadians were delighted. Who wouldn't prefer the romantic adventure of flying to the grim misery of the trenches? The IMB began to manufacture airplanes in Canada. British and Canadian instructors trained more than 10 000 Canadian pilots in 1917 and 1918. By the end of the war, they made up a quarter of the flyers in the Royal Air Force. In 1918, the tiny Canadian Air Force was formed, too late for the war.

Meanwhile, a few Canadians had turned into some of the deadliest killers in the air. A navy pilot, Raymond Collishaw, had the fifth highest score of enemy planes destroyed of any pilot with the British services. William Barker, who won the Victoria Cross, was described as the Royal Air Force's best pilot. No Canadian ever equalled the score of William Bishop, another Victoria Cross winner, who destroyed 72 German planes.

Bishop and many of the other "aces" were not at all like the romantic image of the flying hero. For one thing, Bishop was such a bad pilot that he should probably never have passed flying school. (For that matter, the greatest British ace, Edward Mannock, had only one eye!) Where Bishop excelled was in deadly accuracy with his guns. He also had a killer instinct in the panic confusion of battle and a single-minded passion to add to his score. Like other high-scoring aces, Bishop also knew how to calculate the odds and to clear out of hopeless danger.

Fighting in the air was only the most exciting and novel role for airplanes in the war. By 1918, both the Germans and the British had built huge, two-engined planes that could travel long distances to drop bombs. London and other British cities were bombed and hundreds were killed. The British did the same to German towns. Airplanes were also used to attack troops on the ground, though they were very easy to knock down, and pilots hated that kind of work.

The most important contribution of airplanes was the dull, dangerous work of observing. By 1918, thousands of pictures were taken daily from the air and skilled experts learned how to spot enemy secrets from the faintest of hints on aerial photographs. At sea, airplanes patrolled in front of the British fleet and forced German submarines to waste their short-lived storage batteries by staying underwater.

And everywhere that the British went, from France to the Middle East to North Russia, Canadians flew. By war's end, 22 812 Canadians had served with the British flying services, 7453 as mechanics, the rest as pilots or observers. Of the flyers, 1388 were killed, 1130 were wounded and 377 ended the war as German prisoners.

When this picture was taken in August 1917, Billy Bishop had brought down 37 German planes. By war's end he would have 72 "kills" to rank third among all the aces of the war.

W.A. Bishop, a Canadian from Owen Sound, reports his first "kill": three German Albatros Scouts approached his flight of planes:

"One, separating from the rest, lost height and attempted to come up behind our second to the rear machine. I dived and fired about 12 to 15 rounds. Tracers went all around his machine. He dived steeply to about 600 ft. and flattened out. I followed him and opened fire from 40 to 50 yards range. A group of tracers went into the fuselage and centre section, one being seen to enter directly behind the pilot's seat and one seemed to hit the pilot himself. The machine went out of control in a spinning nose dive. I dived after him firing. I reached 1500 or 2000 ft. My engine had oiled up and I glided just over the line . . . . The Albatros Scout when last seen by me was going vertically downward at a height of 500-600 ft."

From S.F. Wise, *Canadian Airmen and the First World War* (Toronto, 1980)

With 60 victories, Major Raymond Collishaw (left) placed second among Canadian air aces.

One of the unanswered questions of the war is why Canadian flyers did so well, contributing a very high share of the Royal Air Force's victories. Since most Canadian pilots were city-bred, there can be little truth to the popular theory that young men from the Dominion got their edge from an open-air life, cold baths and a lot of practice shooting game.

FOR DISCOVERY

1. Can you suggest any reasons why Canadians should provide far more than their share of Royal Air Force flyers by 1918?
2. Find out about the development of airplanes during the First World War. Would there have been so many changes if there had been no war?
3. Did Canada's role in the air war pay dividends for Canadians when the war was over?
4. Make your own report on what you imagine it would have been like to fly in a First World War dogfight.

An artist's impression of the last flight of the greatest of all air aces, Manfred von Richthofen, the "Red Baron." He is seen closing in on a young Canadian pilot, Lieutenant Wilfrid "Wop" May, seemingly unaware that another Canadian, Captain Ray Brown, is on his tail. The German pilot went down without his eighty-first kill and May survived to become Canada's leading bush pilot after the war. Brown got the credit for the victory but we now know von Richthofen was killed by Australian machine gunners on the ground.

Conscription

In 1917, the war really came home to Canadians. In May, the prime minister announced that men would have to be conscripted—forced to serve—in the Canadian Expeditionary Force. The fight over the Military Service Act split Canadians like no other issue before or since. To make sure that his government's "win-the-war" policy prevailed, Borden gave some women the vote for the first time, took it away from many citizens of foreign birth and formed a Union Government of Conservatives and pro-conscription Liberals.

At the start of 1916, Borden had promised that Canada would send half a million men to the war. By 1917, almost that many had volunteered but there was nonetheless a desperate shortage of Canadian soldiers. When 10 000 were killed or wounded in the fight for Vimy Ridge, they were replaced by raw recruits. Why were there so many volunteers and so few soldiers?

For a start, no one had foreseen how many men were going to become casualties. To keep a division up to strength took 20 000 soldiers a year—and Canada had four divisions. Many of the volunteers were not fit for service, and thousands broke down during training and had to be discharged. Statistics were distorted by men who tried again and again to enlist. One man joined five times and got as far as England twice. He was mentally ill. Another elderly patriot was senile when he reached England.

Moreover, as patriots and recruiting officers kept complaining, there were hundreds of thousands of fit young men who did not volunteer. Many had families or parents to support. By the summer of 1915, there were good jobs for all who wanted them and wages had never been higher. Recruiting propaganda had much more effect on some Canadians than on others. Fighting for King and Empire had little appeal to most French-speaking Quebeckers. Even France was a far-away country that had abandoned Quebec in 1760 and that had forgotten its traditional Catholicism. As for recent immigrants from Europe, often they had come to Canada to escape the threat of war and military service.

From 1915 there was talk of conscription in Canada. Sam Hughes, the Minister of Militia, was opposed. He wanted only the very best in the CEF and he was sure that he could find enough volunteers. By November 1916, his colossal ego led to his dismissal. Borden did not want conscription either. He knew how it would divide Canada. But the facts were too powerful for him. When he went to England and France in March 1917, he learned of the desperate manpower shortage in the Corps. He also learned how badly the war was going for Britain and her Allies. Russia was collapsing and the Tsar had been toppled by revolution. French soldiers had mutinied after being driven into another hopeless offensive. This was not a time

A few first-rate units were raised in Quebec, among them the 163rd *Poil-aux-pattes*. By June 1917, however, only about 13 000 of the 450 000 men and women serving in the CEF were French-speaking.

Jane Walters, then a Canadian nurse in England, remembered her feelings about men who did not volunteer—and those who tried to persuade them:

"Everyone wanted conscription naturally. When you had your own there voluntarily, you hated all those others sitting around having a nice time while yours were being killed. You didn't like them. You'd no respect for them. But I never was one of those who approved of going around handing out white feathers. Do you know that some women did? . . . They actually went to men on the street whom they knew, or if they didn't know them—strong young working men— and handed them a white feather. Of course I nearly died with embarrassment whenever I heard about it."

From Daphne Read (ed.), *The Great War and Canadian Society* (Toronto, 1978)

Some people wanted conscription of wealth before men were taken. This resolution was adopted unanimously in 1916 by the United Farmers of Ontario. In 1919, the UFO formed the Ontario government.

"Since human life is more valuable than gold, this convention most solemnly protests against any proposal looking to the conscription of men for battle while leaving wealth exempt from the same measure of enforced service. It is a manifest and glaring injustice that Canadian mothers should be compelled to surrender boys around whom their dearest hopes in life are centred, while plutocrats, fattening on special privileges and war business, are left in undisturbed possession of their riches."

Henri Bourassa was only Quebec's most prominent and vocal anti-conscriptionist. Most French Canadians shared his conviction that the war was not their concern.

Anti-conscription parade, Victoria Square, Montreal.

for Canada to cut her contribution.

Many Canadians felt otherwise. Resistance was strongest in Quebec where Henri Bourassa, the editor of *Le Devoir,* an influential Montreal newspaper, took the lead. Bourassa argued that Canada should put her own interests first. Her frontiers were not in Flanders but at Halifax. Canadians should give all their energy to creating a prosperous country where both French and English could enjoy full rights. Forcing men to fight was utterly wrong.

These views were so strong in Quebec that the old Liberal leader, Sir Wilfrid Laurier, had to join the anti-conscription fight or see his support vanish. There was quiet support outside Quebec too, especially in the West and the Maritimes, but most of the leaders of English-speaking Canada, Conservative and Liberal, supported Borden's Military Service Act. To increase support, the government made sure that soldiers overseas and their wives, mothers and sisters in Canada could vote. Citizens of "enemy alien" origin were denied the right to vote since, Borden explained, they would be exempt from conscription. By the time Borden's "Union Government" faced election in December 1917, many other men, from soldiers' brothers to farmers' sons, had also been exempted. That helped Borden win a huge majority—almost everywhere but in Quebec.

How did conscription work? All male British subjects were affected. They were divided into classes: first to be called up would be unmarried men between 20 and 34; last would be married men of 40 to 44. Workers in essential occupations, men whose enrolment would cause serious financial, business or family hardship, all clergy and conscientious objectors (such as Mennonites and Doukhobors) could ask for exemption. Local tribunals, with members chosen by the government and the opposition, heard appeals. In the first class, called for January 1, 1918, a full seven months after Borden announced conscription, 93.7 per cent claimed exemption. Local boards allowed 84 per cent of these claims.

Obviously, this was no way to find soldiers. Even worse, in March 1918, the German armies from the Russian front launched a highly successful attack on the British. Using brilliant new tactics on a weak point in the line, the Germans almost destroyed a complete British army. Other attacks followed. On April 19, 1918, Borden rose to announce that exemptions would be cancelled. Over furious opposition from Laurier and challenges in the courts, thousands of conscripts were sent overseas. Many tried to avoid service, hiding in the woods or in abandoned houses. A special police force was organized to pursue them.

When he announced the Military Service bill, Borden said that the CEF hoped to raise a hundred thousand soldiers. By November 11, 1918, there were 99 651 conscripts in the CEF and 24 152 of them were serving with the Canadian Corps in France.

—Perth et Kitchener, c'est-y dans Québec, ça, p'pa ?
—Aw ! Shut-up !

During the 1917 election campaign, English-language newspapers were virtually unanimous in their support of the Union government and conscription. The same could not be said of English-speaking Canadians—as *La Presse*'s cartoonist gleefully pointed out when anti-conscriptionists demonstrated in Perth, Ontario, and Borden was booed off the platform in Kitchener. In fact, conscription was highly unpopular in most rural areas—until, that is, it was announced that farmers' sons would be automatically exempted.

Women serving with the CEF were given the vote in 1917, along with the wives, mothers and sisters of all men who served or had served. These nurses stationed in France were the first women to cast a ballot in a Canadian federal election.

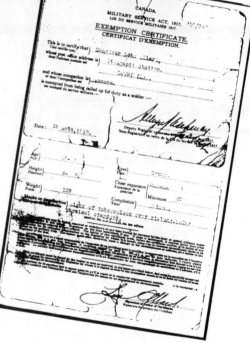

Exemption certificate. By the time the war ended, 401 882 men had been registered as Class I and 221 949 of them had been exempted on medical or occupational grounds.

FOR DISCOVERY

1. Write an argument for or against conscription as you would imagine it being given by (a) a soldier's wife; (b) a French-Canadian worker; (c) someone like you in 1917.
2. Does a country like Canada have the right to make its citizens fight in its wars?
3. Did Sir Robert Borden have any choice in 1917?

Not surprisingly, soldiers voted overwhelmingly for the government in 1917—215 849 to 18 522.

Victory

If anyone had told Canadians in 1918 that the war would soon be over, their answer would have been laughter or, perhaps, anger.

There had been so many promises of victory. Newspapers and magazines regularly told Canadians that the Germans were hungry, unhappy and eager to quit. Instead, it was the Russians who collapsed and, though only a few top leaders knew the full details, it was the French army that refused to fight in 1917. Each offensive promised victory—and produced only huge casualty lists. Worst of all, in 1918, came the German victories. Not even army censors could hide the fact that one of five British armies had collapsed. Other attacks followed until most of the blood-soaked soil captured so painfully by the allies in 1916 and 1917 was in German hands again.

At home in Canada, ordinary Canadians felt the war as they never had before. By 1918, it took a dollar to buy what fifty cents paid for in 1914, and even people with plenty of money could not buy all the food or fuel they wanted. Bad harvests and the need to feed allies and armies overseas led to "war bread," with a fifth of the regular flour replaced by nasty-tasting substitutes. Food items such as sugar that were imported from distant countries, were affected by German submarines. In 1918, the government asked Canadians "on their honour," not to buy more than a pound and a half of sugar per person per month. Butter was also in short supply. Families were asked to buy no more than two pounds a month for each member.

The winter of 1917–18 was one of the harshest anyone could remember. To add to the misery, there was a severe coal shortage. War industries must get what they needed; others had to take their chances. "Gasless Sundays" were added to "fuelless Mondays" and "meatless Fridays" to keep richer Canadians from "joy-riding" in their new cars. Even weekends were not very cheerful.

Certainly Canadians kept trying to "do their bit," but more often now there were government regulations and new officials to see that they were obeyed. Neighbours snooped on neighbours. People accused of hoarding food or coal were arrested and tried. In June 1918, all men and most women were forced to register with the government. People had to report where they were working and whether they would be able to move to jobs that were more important for the war effort.

Because people were fed up with the war, sick of being urged to make sacrifices and angry at "slackers" and others who had done well out of the war, Ottawa and the provinces had to pass more and more rules. Those who believed the fight was against "Prussian militarism" wondered if Canadians were not being given too big a dose of the same kind of medicine.

The British Commander-in-Chief, Sir Douglas Haig, congratulates Canadians after the battle of Amiens, August 1918. In a single day, the Canadians had gone forward thirteen kilometres and taken 5033 prisoners and 161 guns.

The Canadian Motor Machine Gun Corps, with its weapons mounted in heavy trucks, had waited for the open warfare that finally happened in 1918. The last "Hundred Days" was the most costly as well as the most successful Canadian campaign of the war.

Canadian soldiers enter the smouldering ruins of Cambrai, October 11, 1918.

HUMAN COST OF THE WAR

	Total Force Mobilized	Military Deaths	Military Wounded	Civilian Deaths
Allies				
France	8,410,000	1,357,800	4,266,000	40,000
British Empire	8,904,467	908,371	2,090,212	30,633
(Canada)	(619,636)	(60,661)	(144,606)	*
Russia	12,000,000	1,700,000	4,950,000	2,000,000
Italy	5,615,000	462,391	953,886	*
United States	4,355,000	50,585	205,690	*
Belgium	267,000	13,715	44,686	30,000
Serbia	707,343	45,000	133,148	650,000
Montenegro	50,000	3,000	10,000	
Roumania	750,000	335,706	120,000	275,000
Greece	230,000	5,000	21,000	132,000
Portugal	100,000	7,222	13,751	*
Japan	800,000	300	907	*
Total	42,188,810	4,888,891	12,809,280	3,157,633
Central Powers				
Germany	11,000,000	1,808,546	4,247,143	760,000
Austria-Hungary	7,800,000	922,500	3,620,000	300,000
Turkey	2,850,000	325,000	400,000	2,150,000
Bulgaria	1,200,000	75,844	152,390	275,000
Total	22,850,000	3,131,889	8,419,533	3,485,000
Grand total	65,038,810	8,020,780	21,228,813	6,642,633

* Figures not available

SOURCE: *Academic American Encyclopedia*

Captain Elmore Philpott, a soldier who lost his leg in the final months of the war, remembered how the mood changed before the attack at Amiens:

"In the early years of the war the boys used to sing when they went up to the line but then they go into that sort of bleak, blank period and nobody sang. All through that time nobody sang. By some kind of spiritual osmosis or something, when our boys went up to that Amiens thing they all went up singing. There was an entirely different feeling in the air from the minute that we began to move south to go to Amiens. There was a feeling in the air; the boys really believed that this was it."

CBC, "Flanders Field," script 14

44

From Sir Robert Borden to ordinary privates in the CEF or their anxious wives at home, Canadians in 1918 were sure that the war would last another year or two. That was why they thought conscription was necessary. Generals, engineers and scientists worked hard to build new weapons. Meanwhile, soldiers (including Canadians) were sent to Russia to help the Tsar's remaining armies beat down the revolution and get the country back into the war with Germany.

Then, quite suddenly, everything changed. The Canadian Corps had escaped the German attacks of 1918. It was fresh and eager for battle on August 8 when it set out to drive the Germans back from the railway town of Amiens. With the Australians and New Zealanders, the Canadians smashed into the German line. Tanks rolled forward. Overhead, for the first time, airplanes helped smash enemy resistance. In a few days, the Canadians and Australians had driven a huge hole in the German line. General Ludendorf, Germany's top military commander, called August 8 "the black day of the German Army."

Sir Arthur Currie, who commanded the Canadians, could have pushed on, losing many more men. Instead, he arranged to switch the Canadian attack to another sector. Again the four divisions of the Corps won a victory. For the first time, the Germans were reeling back. In fact, they had been worn out by their brilliant attacks of the spring. The Canadians suffered terrible losses but victory made them seem worthwhile. Unlike the Australians, who had run out of volunteers, the Canadian Corps could call on thousands of "MSA" men to fill the ranks. Through September and early October, the Canadians kept pushing, switching and pushing again. To the south, fresh American armies were also winning battles their weary allies had given up expecting.

Among soldiers, spirits soared. At home, a further disaster added to the misery of the year. A terrible worldwide epidemic people called "Spanish Influenza" seems to have begun in India. When it was over, experts claimed that it had killed as many as the war itself. In mid-September 1918, it reached Canada. Hundreds of thousands fell sick. Schools, churches and even businesses closed. There were desperate shortages of beds, medicine, doctors and nurses. The old and frail died, but so did men and women in the prime of life. In a couple of months, at least 10 000 Canadians died from the disease.

Meanwhile, as Canadians struggled with regulations, shortages, influenza and war-weariness, Germany and her allies began to collapse. Turkey, Bulgaria and Austria all abandoned the struggle as revolutions overthrew their governments. By mid-October, German leaders were looking desperately for a way to make peace. When it was ordered to sea in a final, suicide mission, the fleet mutinied. A few days later, the German Kaiser abandoned his throne and fled for safety to neutral Holland. On November 11, 1918, at 11 A.M., the shooting stopped and the war was over.

As the Canadians fight their way through the suburbs of Mons, Belgium, an artilleryman pauses to try to comfort a baby whose mother has been killed by a German shell.

The pipers of the 42nd Highlanders from Montreal march through the Grande Place of Mons, Belgium, on the morning of November 11, 1918.

King St., Toronto, November 11, 1918. News of the armistice reached Canada in the late morning or early afternoon. Across the country, whistles blew, church bells pealed and work stopped as thousands of Canadians took to the streets to celebrate the end of the war.

As part of the British occupying force, the 21st Canadian Infantry Battalion crosses the Rhine at Bonn a few weeks after the armistice.

It was late winter 1919 before all the paperwork was done and transportation organized so that the 350 000 men of the CEF could begin returning home. By July, all but a small remnant were back in Canada.

FOR DISCOVERY

1. Find out from local newspapers how the news of victory came to your community. How did people react?
2. What reasons can you suggest for the government's unwillingness to try rationing by anything more than an "honour" system, even when shortages were expected?
3. Did a new spirit make all the difference when Canadians attacked at Amiens or were there other reasons for their victory?

How did the Spanish Flu affect a town like Sudbury? Here is a report of the local Medical Officer of Health for 1918:

"During the month of October a serious epidemic of Spanish influenza broke out and from the 10th to the 15th we estimated there were some 800 cases. It was deemed advisable . . . that all public premises, schools etc. be closed . . . . A volunteer staff of some 150 men, young women and boys got together and gave valuable assistance to the stricken families; the women doing nursing and caring for the houses, boys doing general errands and chores, and the men found endless work in visiting and helping in many ways. We are greatly indebted to these helpers for their valuable work . . . . The Daughters of the Empire and Red Cross were untiring in the work of making soup and beef-tea for the hospital and invalid patients at their homes . . . ."

After the War

On November 9, 1918, exciting news spread across North America: the war was over. Crowds surged into the streets—only to learn that the reports were only rumours. People were more cautious two days later when huge newspaper headlines announced an end to the fighting. Still, by noon, most Canadians had abandoned work and begun wild celebrations. Civic leaders and clergymen did their best to summon up the words fit to record the end of "the war to end all wars."

Canadians also had to count the cost. Out of 8 million people, more than 60 000 had died in the war. In many parts of Canada, almost every family had suffered loss. Among the soldiers who came home were tens of thousands who were too damaged in body or mind to ever recover fully.

By the summer of 1919, most of Canada's soldiers had come home. Becoming civilians again often proved surprisingly difficult. Politicians had made wonderful-sounding promises of "full re-establishment." What they meant, soldiers discovered, was the good old freedom to work or starve. For able-bodied veterans, there would be no special help to find a home or to improve a rusty skill. Help might hurt their initiative.

Canadians soon tired of veterans and their grumbling. Bankers, businessmen and politicians wanted to get back to normal peacetime methods. Employers wanted to get rid of the trade unions they had often been forced to recognize during the war. The year 1919 was and remains the worst year for labour conflict in Canada's history. When it ended, most unions had suffered a bitter defeat. Farmers got their lesson in 1920, when the wartime Wheat Board was closed and farm prices collapsed. Those who had borrowed when wheat sold at $2 a bushel had to pay off their debts when wheat fetched as little as 60 cents a bushel.

Millions of ordinary Canadians had accepted harsh wartime sacrifices because they believed that victory would make possible a better world and a better Canada. In 1919, many wondered whether it had all been worth it. Veterans found that they were among the few people who had not shared in wartime wage increases. Workers and farmers believed that rich Canadians had profited enormously from the war.

Overseas, when the allies met at Versailles to make a permanent peace, the great powers were soon at odds, while the many small nationalities liberated by the war pursued their own bitter quarrels. By their harsh treatment of Germany and other defeated enemies, the victors also laid the foundations for another, even more terrible world war only 20 years later.

Most Canadians wanted to forget about the world, idealism and sacrifice. They had had enough of them all during the war years. Like most people after a period of dramatic change, they were weary and a little disappointed.

What a contrast with the mood in 1914!

THAT FIRST CIVIE COLLAR.

An Ontario farmer's son, Fred Heasman, reflected the restlessness of most discharged veterans:

"I helped Dad around the farm. I wasn't really happy, though I was glad to be out of the army. But you had been so used to going all the time and there was always a crowd, a gang. It just seemed so quiet, I didn't know what to do with myself . . . .

I went up to Toronto and took a train west. I worked for about two weeks faithfully. I enjoyed myself and earned five dollars a day—a lot more money than ever before. But rain and snow started and held us up for two weeks. I just couldn't take it, so I caught the first train to Winnipeg and came back to Toronto.

I had to get a job, but didn't have any luck the first day. I remember one of the fellows saying, "Well, you won't get a job here. Take that damned button off." I had a button that they gave to veterans. Employers were having so much trouble with veterans. They just wouldn't stay. For a lot of us it was nerves. We had been under high tension for too long. So the next day I took my button off."

From William D. Mathieson, *My Grandfather's War* (Toronto, 1981)

The Vimy Memorial, completed in 1936, stands on the highest point of Vimy Ridge. On its walls are inscribed the names of the 11 285 Canadian soldiers who were posted as "missing, presumed dead" in France.

Two full years after the war ended, more than 6500 veterans were still in hospital.

IN THE NAME OF GOD
WHAT IS THERE
FOR **US** TO BE
THANKFUL FOR?

Unemployed veterans march in Toronto. Many returned soldiers were understandably bitter. As one put it, "the ex-soldier . . . knows that he has seen comrades fall beside him and he was taking the same chances they were, yet the dead are heroes . . . . They are publicly acclaimed while he tramps the streets searching in vain for a job that will keep body and soul together. The living are almost outcasts."

FOR DISCOVERY

1. How would you explain the restlessness of former soldiers such as Fred Heasman?
2. What sort of help should Canada have offered its returned soldiers in 1919? Was the government right to avoid helping the able-bodied men to "re-establish" themselves?
3. What was the lasting effect of the First World War on Canada? You might look at some specific area, such as industry, agriculture, government services or social attitudes.
4. Was the First World War worth it for Canada?

Selected Further Reading

Berger, Carl. *Conscription, 1917*. Toronto: University of Toronto Press, 1969. A collection of articles on all aspects of the conscription question.

Bird, W.R. *Ghosts Have Warm Hands*. Toronto: Clarke Irwin, 1976. One of the best accounts by any participant in the war of what the fighting was like for individual soldiers.

Bliss, Michael. *A Canadian Millionaire: The Life and Business Times of Sir Joseph Flavelle, 1858–1939*. Toronto: Macmillan, 1978. This biography of the head of the Imperial Munitions Board provides a good look at Canada's munitions industry.

English, John. *Borden: His Life and World*. Toronto: McGraw–Hill Ryerson, 1977. A general yet detailed survey of the social, political and economic realities of Canada from the turn of the century to 1921.

Goodspeed, D.J. *The Road Past Vimy: The Canadian Corps, 1914–1918*. Toronto: Macmillan, 1969. A short, readable analysis of Canadian military operations in the First World War.

Morton, Desmond. *A Peculiar Kind of Politics*. Toronto: University of Toronto Press, 1982. A view of Canada's growth to self-government during the war years.

———. *Years of Conflict 1911–1921*. Toronto: Grolier Limited, 1983. A taut but well-balanced analytical account of events in Canada and the international arena before, during and after World War I.

Read, Daphne (ed.). *The Great War and Canadian Society: An Oral History*. Toronto: New Hogtown Press, 1978. This book provides interesting insights into how the war affected Canadians, but the reader must remember that it is based on people's memories over half a century—not always the most accurate evidence.

Swettenham, John. *Canada and the First World War*. Toronto: McGraw–Hill Ryerson, 1973. A solid, clearly written account of the services of the Canadian Corps overseas.

Wise, S.F. *Canadian Airmen and the First World War*. Toronto: University of Toronto Press, 1980. A recent, very detailed history of the newest dimension of war.

Illustration Credits

Abbreviations: T—top; M—middle; B—bottom; L—left; R—right.

Cover: *Stretcher Bearers* by H.J. Mowat, courtesy Canadian War Museum/National Museum of Man/National Museums of Canada (CWM), acc. no. 8567; p. 4: Metro Toronto Library Board (MTLB); p. 5 T: Public Archives of Canada (PAC) PA27012; M: PAC WS-54; B: Ontario Archives (OA); p. 6 T: PAC PA22739; B: PAC 107281; p. 7 T: City of Toronto Archives (CTA); M, B: OA; p. 8 T: PAC PA4836; B: PAC PA91096; p. 9 T: OA; M: MTLB; B: CTA; p. 10 TL: PAC C95374; TR: PAC C95748; ML: PAC C42420; MR: PAC C14095; B: MTLB; p. 11 T: CTA; B: Manitoba Archives (MA); p. 12: PAC C42857; p. 13 T: MTLB; M: PAC; B: CTA; p. 14: MTLB; p. 15 T: MTLB; M: MA; B: CTA; p. 16 T: PAC C21066; B: British Columbia Archives (BCA); p. 17 T: BCA; B: PAC C81360; p. 18 T: PAC PA24516; B: PAC PA24562; p. 19 T: PAC PA24590; B: PAC PA24439; p. 20 T: PAC PA24609; M: PAC PA24363; B: PAC PA24456; p. 21 M: PAC TC568; B: CTA; p. 22 M: Department of National Defence (DND); B: PAC C107237; p. 23 T: OA; ML: PAC PA292; MR: OA; B: PAC PA1050; p. 24 T: PAC PA832; M: MTLB; B: PAC; p. 25 T: PAC PA2045; M: DND; B: OA; p. 26 M: OA; B: OA; p. 27 T: PAC PA648; M: PAC PA826; BR: PAC PA1017; p. 28 T: PAC PA2084; M: PAC PA2777; B: PAC PA2515; p. 29 T: OA; ML: PAC PA2296; MR: DND; B: PAC PA4352; p. 30 T: PAC PA1439; B: PAC PA3231; p. 31 T: OA; M: PAC PA1355; B: OA; p. 32 T: PAC PA1660; PAC; p. 33 T: OA; M: OA; B: PAC PA880; p. 34 T: PAC C20396; B: PAC PA2722; p. 35 T: PAC PA4652; M: DND; B: OA; p. 36 T: PAC PA1654; p. 37 T: PAC; B: Royal Canadian Military Institute (RCMI); p. 38: PAC C95733; p. 39 T: PAC C4956; B: PAC C6859; p. 40 T: PAC C9031; M: OA; B: PAC C9021; p. 41 T: PAC PA2279; M: MTLB; B: OA; p. 42 T: PAC PA2900; B: OA; p. 43: OA; p. 44 T: PAC PA3539; M: A; B: OA; p. 45: OA; p. 46: MTLB; p. 47 T: OA; M: CTA; B: Department of Veterans' Affairs.